Expository Nuggets from 1 Peter
26 Sermon Outlines on Triumphant Living

Patrick Mead
Machaira Touch Ministries, Inc.

© 2008 by Machaira Touch Ministries
All rights reserved.

ISBN 978-0-6152-0068-2

Printed in the United States of America.

Acknowledgements

This work is dedicated to my wife, Christy, who is the greatest encouragement I have for the kingdom work that God has called me to do. I am also thankful for the believers at Willow Springs Baptist Church in Athens, Texas where these sermons were prepared and preached.

Preface

My library shelves are filled with books on sermon outlines, and those books are just a few that are available to preachers and teachers today. Why, on earth, would I want to provide another book on sermon outlines, when there are so many already available at present?

The reason I have so many books on sermon outlines is the reason I want to provide another. Ideas beget ideas. The more ideas you have the more ideas you can produce. It is a never ending cycle. There has been many times where God used someone else's outline to create my own outline on a passage that I was working on. This is the main reason I have provided these outlines from 1 Peter.

These outlines are only useful if you study the passage. I have purposely left bare bones on these outlines so that there will be no temptation to forgo the process of studying the word of God. I believe that a preacher needs to have an encounter with the truth if he wants his people to have an encounter with the truth. This encounter takes place in the hallowed study.

When you study the passage you will begin to see these outlines come to life. You will notice that they are directly from the text so you should find no surprises between the text and the outline.

For these outlines to have any value there needs to be two things take place. First, there needs to be the fire of conviction from the preacher. This fire can only come from the fuel of the word of God. Therefore, you need to study.

Second, there needs to be the power of the Holy Spirit upon the preacher. I don't care how polished your sermon is, or how nice of an outline you have to communicate the truth, unless you have received power from the Holy Spirit your labor will be in vain. May God abundantly empower both your study time and your pulpit time for his glory and his glory alone.

Dr. Patrick Mead
Machaira Touch Ministries, Inc.

Contents

Part 1	**The Foundation for Triumphant Living (1:1-1:12)**	5
1	The Privileged Position of Believers (1:1-2)	6
2	The Great Salvation of Believers (1:3-5)	7
3	The Paradoxical Experiences of Believers (1:6-9)	8
4	The Magnitude of the Salvation of Believers (1:10-12)	9
Part 2	**The Fundamentals for Triumphant Living (1:13-2:3)**	10
5	A Life of Constant Hope (1:13)	11
6	A Life of Constant Holiness (1:14-16)	12
7	A Life of Constant Fear (1:17-21)	14
8	A Life of Constant Love (1:22-25)	15
9	A Life of Constant Growth (2:1-3)	16
Part 3	**The Position of Triumphant Living (2:4-10)**	17
10	A People of Worship (2:4-5)	18
11	A People of Destiny (2:6-8)	20
12	A People of Purpose (2:9-10)	22
Part 4	**The Witness of Triumphant Living (2:11-3:12)**	23
13	Witnessing without Words (2:11-12)	24

14	Witnessing without Words as Citizens (2:13-17)	25
15	Witnessing by Submitting to Authority (2:18-25)	26
16	The Witness of a Christian Wife (3:1-6)	28
17	The Witness of a Christian Husband (3:7)	30
18	The Witness of a Christian Community (3:8-12)	32

Part 5 **The Suffering of Triumphant Living (3:13-5:14)** **34**

19	Dealing with Undeserved Trouble (3:13-17)	35
20	Encouragement for Suffering Christians (3:18-22)	37
21	No Compromise Christians (4:1-6)	39
22	Living with the End in View (4:7-11)	40
23	Steadfast in the Midst of Suffering (4:12-19)	41
24	What it Takes to be a Pastor (5:1-4)	42
25	Humility and the Household of Faith (5:5-7)	43
26	The Forgotten War (5:8-14)	44

Part 1

The Foundation for Triumphant Living
1 Peter 1:1-12

The Privileged Position of Believers
1 Peter 1:1-2

I. The privileged position of the believer (1)

    a. Spiritual position: *"who are chosen"*

    b. Social position: *"aliens"*

II. The foundation for the privileged position (2)

    a. The source of the privilege position (2a)

    b. The means of making the privileged position effective (2b)

    c. The aim and purpose of making the privileged position effective (2c)

The Great Salvation of Believers
1 Peter 1:3-5

I. The source of salvation (3)

    a. The mercy of God the Father

    b. The resurrection of God the Son

II. The substance of salvation (3b-4a)

    a. A living hope (3b)

    b. A lasting inheritance (4a)

        i. Lasting in substance "imperishable"

        ii. Lasting in purity "undefiled"

        iii. Lasting in beauty "not fade away"

III. The security of salvation (4b-5)

    a. The security of the inheritance (4b)

    b. The security of the inheritor (5)

The Believer's Paradoxical Experience
1 Peter 1:6-9

I.   The paradoxical experience of joy (6-7)

    a. The joy expressed (6a)

    b. The paradox experienced (6b)

        i Present trials "now."

        ii Passing trials "for a little while"

        iii Purposeful trials "If need be"

    c. The outcome expected (7)

II.   The paradoxical experience of love (8-9)

    a. The love expressed (8a)

    b. The paradox encountered (8b)

    c. The present experience (9)

The Magnitude of the Believer's Salvation
1 Peter 1:10-12

I. The diligent search of the Old Testament prophets (10-12a)

    a. The service of the prophets (10a)

    b. The source of the prophecy (11a)

    c. The substance of the search

        i The aim of the search (10b, 11b)

        ii The result of the search (12a)

II. The divine inquiry of the heavenly multitude (12b)

Part 2

Fundamentals for Triumphant Living
1Peter 1:13-2:3

A Life of Constant Hope
1 Peter 1:13

I. The call to live a life of constant hope (13b)

    a. The call to hope "fix your hope"

    b. The object of hope "on the grace…"

II. The condition for living a life of constant hope (13a)

    a. The proper attitude for hope "prepare your minds"

    b. The proper discipline for hope "be sober"

Life of Constant Holiness
1 Peter 1:14-16

I. The premise for a life of holiness (14a)

    a. The nature of our relationship "children"

    b. The description of our relationship "obedient"

II. The prohibition for a life of holiness (14b)

    a. The prohibition to follow

    b. The standards to avoid

III. The petition for a life of holiness (15b)

    a. The exhortation to holiness

    b. The extent of holiness "in all your behavior"

IV. The purpose for a life of holiness (15a, 16)

   a. Theological purpose (15a)

   b. The Biblical proof (16)

A Life of Constant Fear
1 Peter 1:17-21

I. The command that invokes a life of fear (17)

    a. The circumstances for a life of fear (17a)

        i. The relationship with the Father

        ii. The position of the Father

    b. The command for a life of fear (17b)

        i. The command to fear

        ii. The duration of fear

II. The knowledge that inspires a life of fear (18-21)

    a. The costly price of redemption (18-19)

    b. The divine purpose of redemption (20)

    c. The divine affirmation of redemption (21)

A Life of Constant Love
1 Peter 1:22-25

I. The situation that generates a life of love (22a)

    a. The reality of purification

    b. The purpose of purification

II. The summons to live a life of love (22b)

    a. The summons to love

    b. The source of love

III. The support for a life of love (23-25)

    a. The reality of regeneration (23a)

    b. The means of regeneration (23b)

    c. The permanence of regeneration (24-25)

A Life of Constant Growth
1 Peter 2:1-3

I. Remove the hindrances to spiritual growth (1)

    a. The essential to embrace (1a)

    b. The encumbrances to eliminate (1b)

II. Hunger for the source of spiritual growth (2)

    a. The hunger for the source (2b)

    b. The illustration of the hunger (2a)

    c. The purpose for the hunger (2c)

III. Remember the incentive for spiritual growth (3)

    a. The certainty of the incentive (3a)

    b. The composition of the incentive (3b)

Part 3

The Position of Triumphant Living
1 Peter 2:4-10

A People of Worship
Offering Acceptable Worship
1 Peter 2:4-5

I. The strategy of acceptable worship (4a)

   a. The strategy "coming"

   b. The target "to Him"

   c. The motive (3b) "tasted"

II. The objective of acceptable worship (5a)

   a. The increasing presence of God "built up…"

   b. The effect of God's increasing presence "holy priesthood"

III. The purpose of acceptable worship (5b)

   a. The Purpose "spiritual sacrifices"

      i. Our person

        ii. Our possessions

        iii. Our praises

        iv. Our practice

IV.   The source of acceptable worship (5c)

     a. The source "through Jesus Christ"

A People of Destiny
1 Peter 2:6-8

I. The destiny of the believer: e*xoneration* (6-7a)

    a. The precious attitude of the believer towards Jesus (7a)[1]

    b. The precious position of the believer (7a)[2]

    c. The precious destiny of the believer (6b,7a)
The value of Jesus before the Father is given to those who believe on his name. Therefore, the believer can be sure than when he or she stands before God, God will see them as he sees Jesus.

II. The destiny of the unbeliever: *condemnation* (7b-8)

    a. The foolish assumption: unimportant (7c)
The foolish assumption is found in the quote from Psalm 118 that Peter uses to make the contrast.

---

[1] This point is brought out from the New King James

[2] This point is brought out from the New American Standard

b. The foolish assertion: unbelief (8b)
   What is the foolish assertion? It is found in the latter part of verse eight: "disobedient to the word."

c. The fatal destiny: condemnation (8a)

A People of Purpose
1 Peter 2:9-10

I. The identity of the people of God (9a)

    a. Chosen Race

    b. Royal Priesthood

    c. Holy Nation

    d. A People of Possession

II. The purpose of the people of God (9b-10)

    a. The purpose (9b)

    b. The message (10)

    c. The method

        i. Word

        ii. Walk

Part 4

The Witness of Triumphant Living
1 Peter 2:11-3:12

Witnessing Without Words
1 Peter 2:11-12

I. Remember your position in the world (11a)

    a. The position in the world "aliens and strangers"

    b. The position in the kingdom

II. Conform you conduct to your position (11b-12a)

    a. Inward conformity (11b)

    b. Outward conformity (12a)

III. Realize the purpose of your witness (12b)

    a. Challenge the misconceptions of unbelievers "slander you"

    b. Give consistent witness for unbelievers "good deeds…observe"

    c. Lead unbelievers to a saving response "glorify God"

Witnessing Without Words as Citizens
2:13-17

I. The mandate for witnessing without words as citizens (13-14)

   a. The mandate (13a)

   b. The scope (13b-14)

II. The incentive for witnessing without words as citizens (13a, 15)

   a. Honors the Lord (13a) "The Lord's sake"

   b. Fulfills the Lord's will (15)

III. The attitude for witnessing without words as citizens (16)

IV. The limitations for witnessing without words as citizens (17)

Witnessing by Submitting to Authority
1 Peter 2:18-25

I. The expectation of submission to authority (18)

    a. The command for submission "submissive"

    b. The quality of submission "respect"

    c. The scope of submission "unreasonable"

II. The endorsement of submission to authority (19-20)

    a. The condition (19)

    b. The contrast (20)

III. The example of submission to authority (21-25)

    a. The basis for submission (21a)

    b. The example of submission (21b-22)

    c. The purpose of submission (24-25)

        i. Redemption (24a)

        ii. Righteousness (24b)

        iii. Reconciliation (25)

The Witness of a Christian Wife
1 Peter 3:1-6

I. A witness in the marriage life (1-2)

    a. The precept

        i. The connection "in the same way"

        ii. The command "be submissive"

        iii. The consistency: explain the relevance for today

    b. The predicament

        i. The husbands condition "disobedient to the word"

    c. The purpose (1b-2)

        i. The purpose of redemption "won"

        ii. The process of redemption "observe"

II. A witness of the inner life (3-4)

    a. The external (3)

    b. The internal (4)

III. A witness of a biblical life (5-6)

   a. A devout life (5)

   b. A biblical life (6)

The Witness of the Christian Husband
1 Peter 3:7

I. The principles to emulate (7a)

    a. The knowledge principle "understanding way"

        i. Biblical knowledge

        ii. Biological knowledge

    b. The honor principle "show her honor"

        i. The explanation of the honor principle

            1. Physical differences

            2. Positional differences

            3. Emotional differences

        ii. The application of the honor principle

    c. The equality principle "fellow heir"

II. The purpose to encourage (7b)

    a. The incentive of prayer

    b. The incentive of fellowship

The Witness of a Christian Community
1 Peter 3:8-12

I. Demonstrate a righteous activity within the community (8-9a)

    a. The admonition to the community "all of you"

    b. The righteous attitudes of the community

        i. Harmonious attitude

        ii. Sympathetic attitude

        iii. Loving attitude

        iv. Compassionate attitude

        v. Humble attitude

    c. The righteous actions of the community

        i. The unrighteous actions to avoid "not returning"

        ii. The righteous actions to appropriate "giving a blessing"

II. Imitate the righteous King of the community (9b)

       a. The calling to imitate "called for the very purpose"

       b. The blessing to inherit "inherit a blessing"

III.   Supported by the righteous confirmation upon the community (10-12)

       a. The righteous ambition suggested (10a)

       b. The righteous activities supported (10b-11)

       c. The righteous affirmation supported (12)

Part 5

The Suffering of Triumphant Living
1 Peter 3:13-5:14

Dealing with Undeserved Troubles
1 Peter 3:13-17

I. Christians will encounter undeserved troubles (13-14a)

    a. No one expects to be mistreated for doing good (13)

    b. There are times when doing good will solicit undeserved troubles (14a)

        i. The trouble explained "But even if you should suffer"

        ii. The cause of the trouble "righteousness sake"

    c. It is a blessing when Christians face undeserved troubles "you are blessed"

II. Christians can endure undeserved troubles (14b-16)

    a. Do not fear those who trouble you (14b)

    b. Remember Christ's Lordship (15a)

    c. Be prepared to share the hope of Jesus Christ (15b)

        d. Let your behavior speak of the hope of Jesus Christ (16)

III.   Christians can be encouraged by undeserved troubles(17)

        a. It is God's will

        b. It is God's way

        c. It is God's work

Encouragement for Suffering Christians
1 Peter 3:18-22

I. The example of Christ (18)

    a. Christ's suffering was in accordance with the will of God

    b. Christ's suffering was in accordance with the way of God

        i. Because of the why he died "for sin"

        ii. Because of how he died: "redemption through his blood"[3]

    c. Christ's suffering was in accordance with the work of God "bring us to God"

---

[3] Ephesians 1:7

II. The empowerment of Christ (19-21)

    a. Support for the Christian witness (19)

    b. Security for the Christian witness (20-21)

III. The enthronement of Christ (22)

No Compromise Christians
1 Peter 4:1-6

I. The insight needed to be a no compromise Christian (1-2)

    a. The object of insight (1a)

    b. The objective of insight (1b)

    c. The outcome (2)

II. The incentives given to be a no compromise Christian (3-6)

    a. The past incentive (3)

    b. The present incentive (4)

    c. The prospective incentive (5-6)

Living with the End in View
1 Peter 4:7-11

I. Comprehend the theological truth of Christ's return (7a)

II. Carry out the practical implications of Christ's return (7b-11a)

    a. Inferred implications "therefore"

    b. Prayerful implications (7b)

    c. Ministry implications (8-11a)

        i. The exhortation for community living (8)

        ii. The application in community living (9-11a)

III. Concentrate on the goal of carrying out the practical implications (11b)

Steadfast in the Midst of Suffering
1 Peter 4:12-19

I. The necessary perspective (12-13a)

    a. Understand God's purpose for trials (12)

    b. Obey God's proposal in trials (13a) "keep on rejoicing"

II. The bestowed privilege (13b-16)

    a. The privilege confirmed (14,16)

    b. The privilege clarified (15)

    c. The privilege conferred (13b)

III. The intentional purification (17-18)

    a. The present process of purification (17a)

    b. The pending process of purification (17b-18)

IV. The fundamental practice (19)

    a. Trust in the faithful Creator "entrust their souls"

    b. Obey the faithful Creator "doing what is right"

What it Takes to be a Pastor
1 Peter 5:1-4

I. The position of pastor has a spiritual requisition (1)

    a. The spiritual position[4]

    b. The spiritual requisition[5]

II. The position of pastor has a specific responsibility (2-3)

    a. The exhortation to the specific responsibility (2a)

    b. The explanation of the specific responsibility (2b-3)

III. The position of pastor has a special reward (4)

---

[4] I would bring out both the position of elder/pastor and the spiritual maturity needed for the position.

[5] In John 21:16, Jesus says to Peter, *"shepherd my sheep."* The same command that Jesus gives to Peter is the same command that Peter gives to pastors in 1 Peter 5:1. The same imperative verb is used in both places the only difference is that the one given to Peter is second person singular, the one given to the pastors is second person plural. Who called Peter to "shepherd my sheep?" It was the Lord Jesus. The same Lord Jesus that gave Peter a spiritual requisition to be a pastor is the same Lord Jesus that calls men to be pastors today.

Humility and the Household of Faith
1 Peter 5:5-7

I. Humility and how it relates to the leadership (5a)

II. Humility and how it relates to the laity (5b)

III. Humility and how it relates to the Lord (6-7)

    a. The imperative (6)

    b. The method (7)

The Forgotten War
1 Peter 5:8-11

I. The attentive outlook concerning the foe (8)

    a. The command in light of the foe (8a)

    b. The character of the foe (8b)

II. The active opposition concerning the fight (9)

III. The assured outcome concerning the finish (10-11)

www.ingramcontent.com/pod-product-compliance
Lightning Source LLC
Chambersburg PA
CBHW031436040426
42444CB00006B/836